Essential Jazz Guitar Chords

William Bay

Cover image of the Frank Vignola model FV680CE-SB guitar is courtesy of Eastman Music Company.

Table of Contents

Table of Contents

How to Read Chord Diagrams

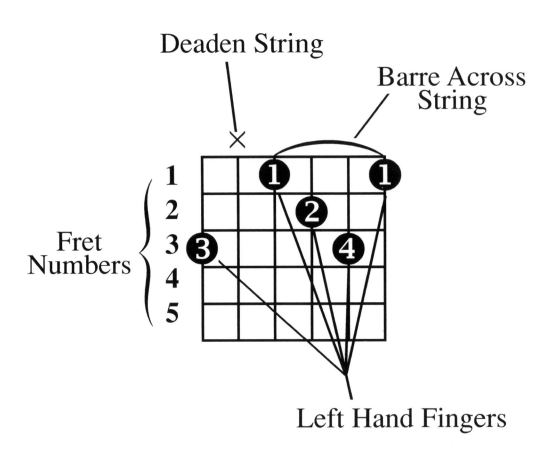

Major Chords

C

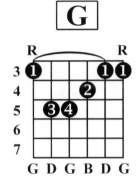

Major Chords

A

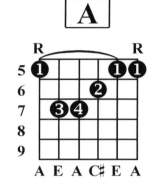

G   **D**

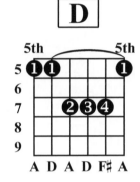

E   **B**

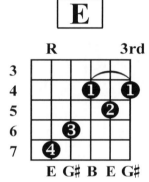
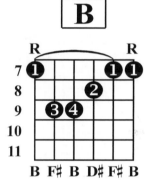

Major Chords

G♭/F♯

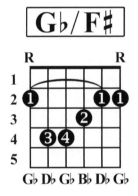

D♭   **A♭**

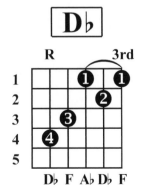
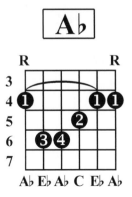

Major Chords

E♭

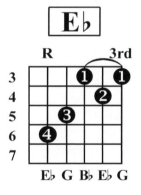

B♭   **F**

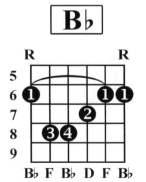
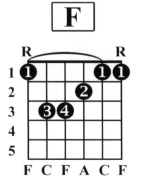

Minor Chords

Cm

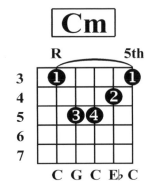

Gm   Dm

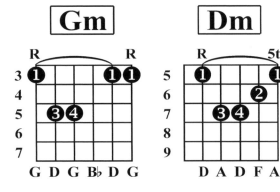

Minor Chords

Am

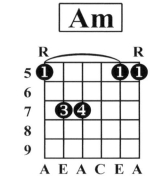

Em   Bm

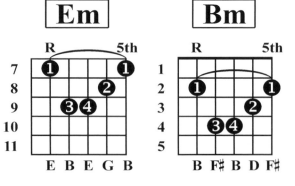

Minor Chords

G♭m / F#m

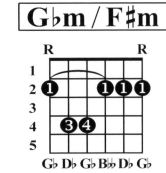

D♭m   A♭m

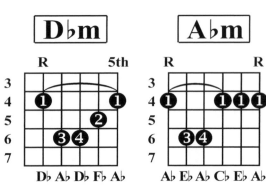

Minor Chords

E♭m

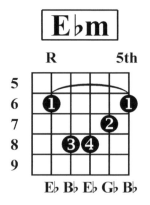

B♭m   Fm

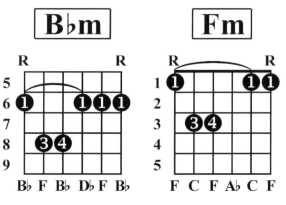

Dominant Seventh

Dominant Seventh

C7

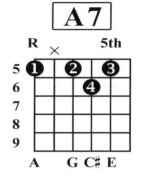

A7

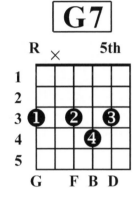

G7

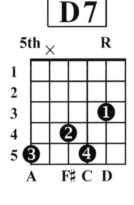

D7

E7

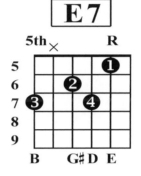

B7

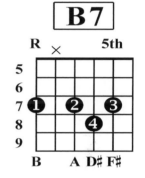

Dominant Seventh

Dominant Seventh

G♭7 / F♯7

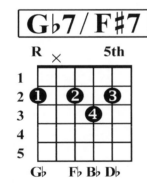

E♭7

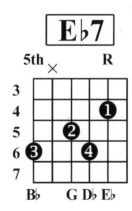

D♭7

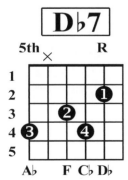

A♭7

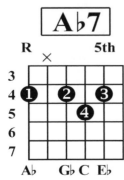

B♭7

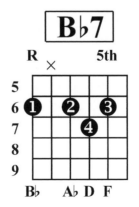

F7

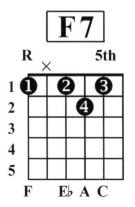

Major Seventh

Cma7

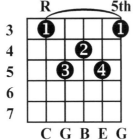

Gma7

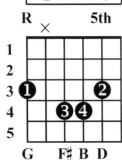

Dma7

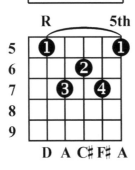

Major Seventh

G♭ma7 / F♯ma7

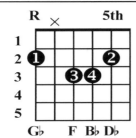

D♭ma7

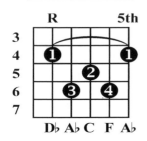

A♭ma7

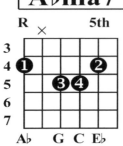

Major Seventh

Ama7

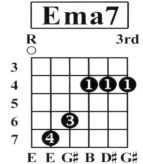

Ema7

Bma7

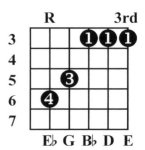

Major Seventh

E♭ma7

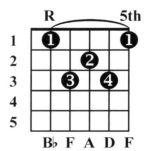

B♭ma7

Fma7

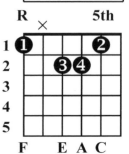

Major Sixth

Major Sixth

C6

A6

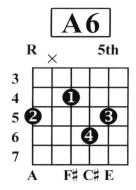

G6

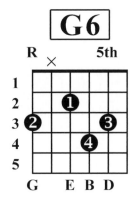

D6

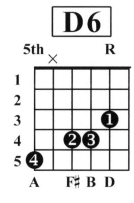

E6

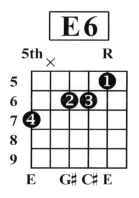

B6

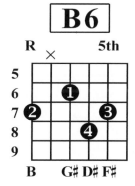

Major Sixth

Major Sixth

G♭6 / F♯6

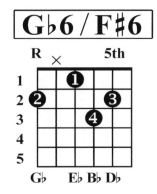

E♭6

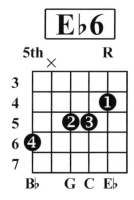

D♭6

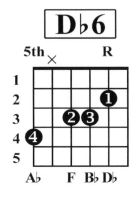

A♭6

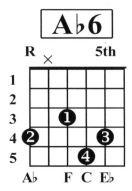

B♭6

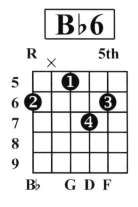

F6

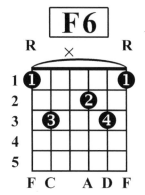

9

Minor Seventh

Cm7

Am7
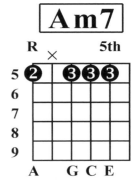

Gm7
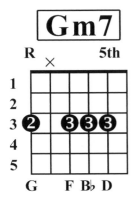

Dm7
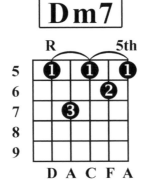

Minor Seventh

Em7
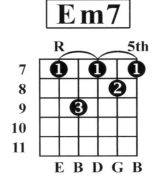

Bm7
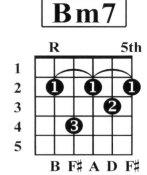

Minor Seventh

G♭m7/F♯m7
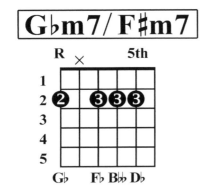

D♭m7
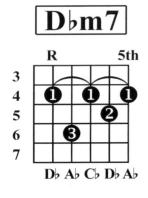

A♭m7
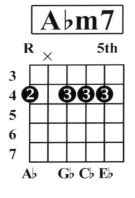

Minor Seventh

E♭m7
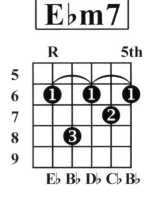

B♭m7
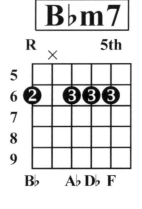

Fm7
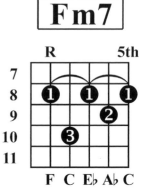

10

Minor Sixth

Cm6

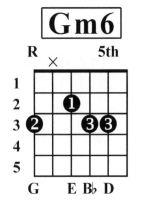

Gm6

Dm6

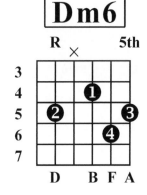

Minor Sixth

Am6

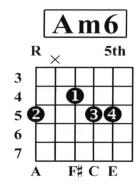

Em6

Bm6

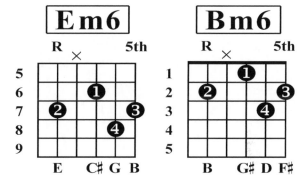

Minor Sixth

G♭m6 / F♯m6

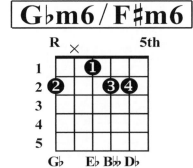

D♭m6

A♭m6

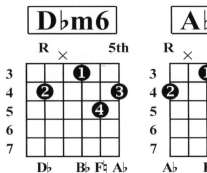
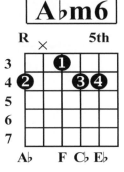

Minor Sixth

E♭m6

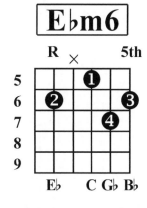

B♭m6

Fm6

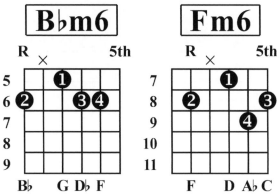

11

7th Suspended 4th

C7sus

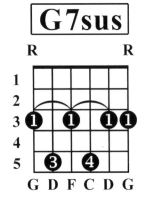

G7sus

D7sus

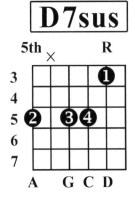

7th Suspended 4th

A7sus

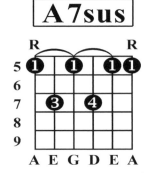

E7sus

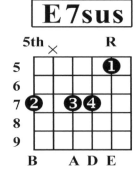

B7sus

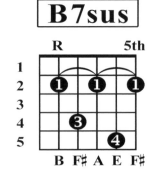

7th Suspended 4th

Gb7sus / F#7sus

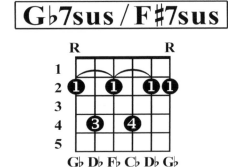

Db7sus

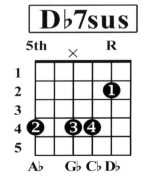

Ab7sus

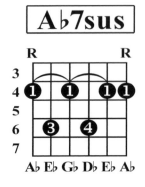

7th Suspended 4th

Eb7sus

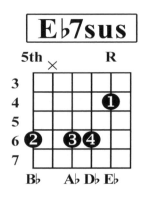

Bb7sus

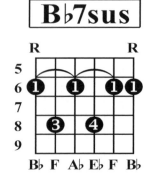

F7sus

Diminished #1

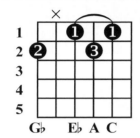

$C^\circ, E\flat^\circ, G\flat^\circ, A^\circ$

G♭ E♭ A C

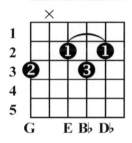

$D\flat^\circ, E^\circ, G^\circ, B\flat^\circ$

G E B♭ D♭

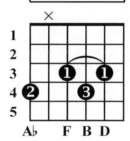

$D^\circ, F^\circ, A\flat^\circ, B^\circ$

A♭ F B D

Diminished #2

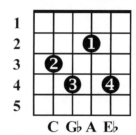

$C^\circ, E\flat^\circ, G\flat^\circ, A^\circ$

C G♭ A E♭

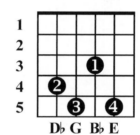

$D\flat^\circ, E^\circ, G^\circ, B\flat^\circ$

D♭ G B♭ E

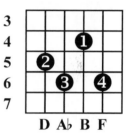

$D^\circ, F^\circ, A\flat^\circ, B^\circ$

D A♭ B F

Augmented

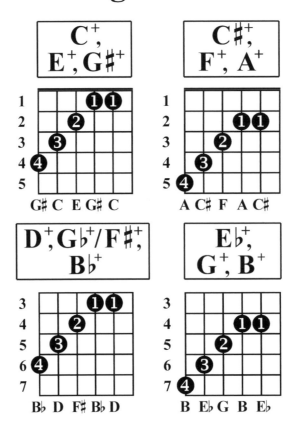

Major-Minor 7th

Cma-mi7

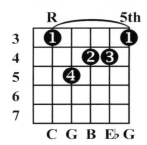

Gma-mi7

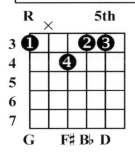

Dma-mi7

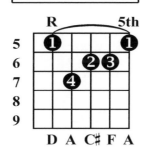

Major-Minor 7th

Ama-mi7

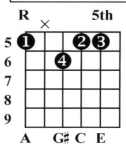

Ema-mi7

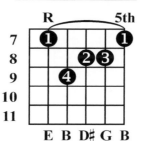

Bma-mi7

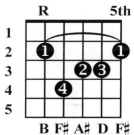

Major-Minor 7th

G♭ma-mi7 / F♯ma-mi7

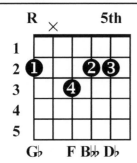

D♭ma-mi7

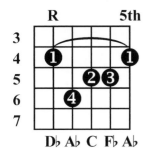

A♭ma-mi7

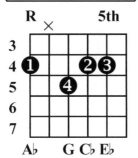

Major-Minor 7th

E♭ma-mi7

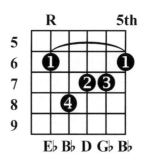

B♭ma-mi7

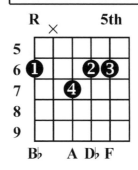

Fma-mi7

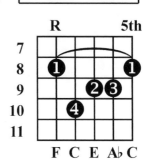

15

7♯5

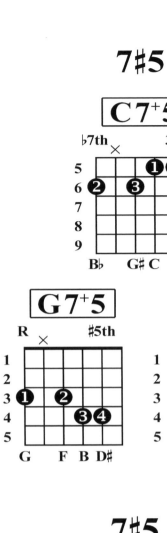
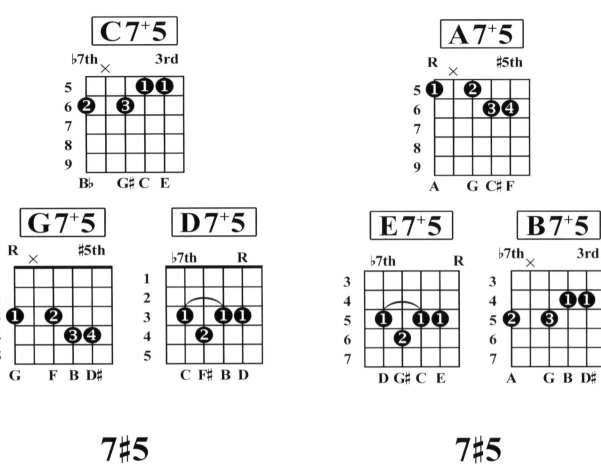

7♯5

7♯5

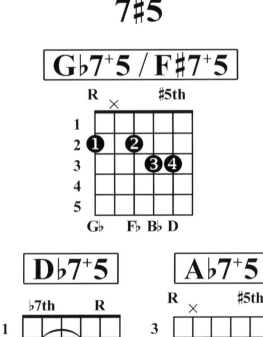
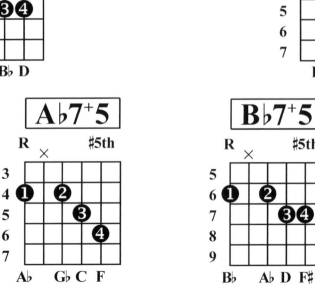
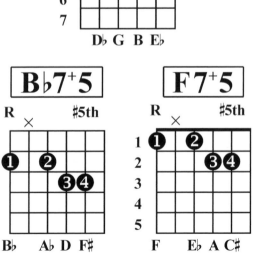

7♭5

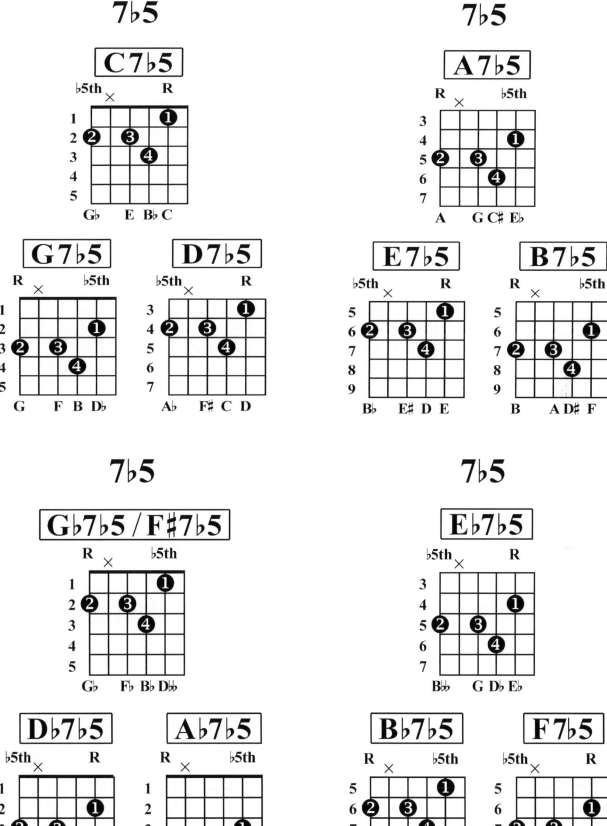

7♭5

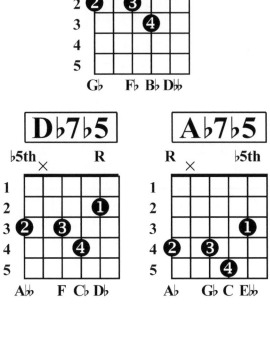

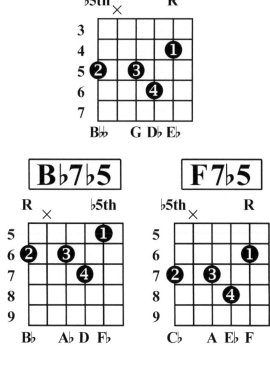

Minor7♭5
Half-Diminished

Cm7♭5
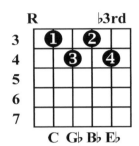

R   ♭3rd

C G♭ B♭ E♭

Gm7♭5
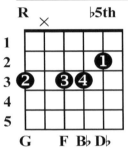

R   ×   ♭5th

G   F B♭ D♭

Dm7♭5
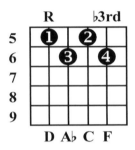

R   ♭3rd

D A♭ C F

Minor7♭5
Half-Diminished

Am7♭5
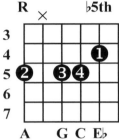

R   ×   ♭5th

A   G C E♭

Em7♭5
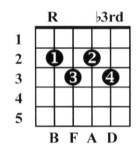

♭5th ×   R

B♭   G D E

Bm7♭5

R   ♭3rd

B F A D

Minor7♭5
Half-Diminished

G♭m7♭5 / F♯m7♭5
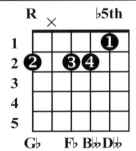

R   ×   ♭5th

G♭   F♭ B♭♭ D♭♭

D♭m7♭5

R   ♭3rd

D♭ A♭♭ C♭ F♭

A♭m7♭5

R   ×   ♭5th

A♭   G♭ C E♭♭

Minor7♭5
Half-Diminished

E♭m7♭5
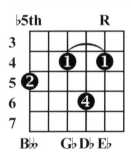

♭5th   R

B♭♭   G♭ D♭ E♭

D♭m7♭5

R   ×   ♭5th

B♭   A♭ D♭ F♭

Fm7♭5

♭5th ×   R

C♭   A♭ E♭ F

18

Ninth

C9

G9

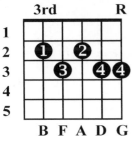

D9

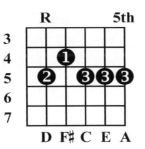

Ninth

A9

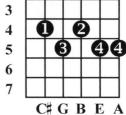

E9

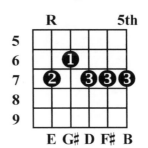

B9

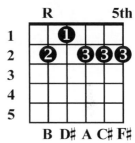

Ninth

Gb9 / F#9

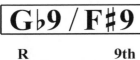
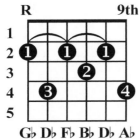

Db9

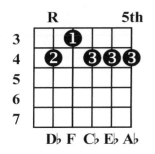

Ab9

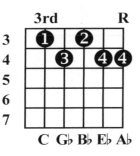

Ninth

Eb9

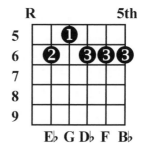

Bb9

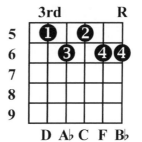

F9

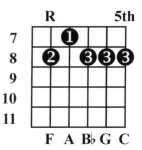

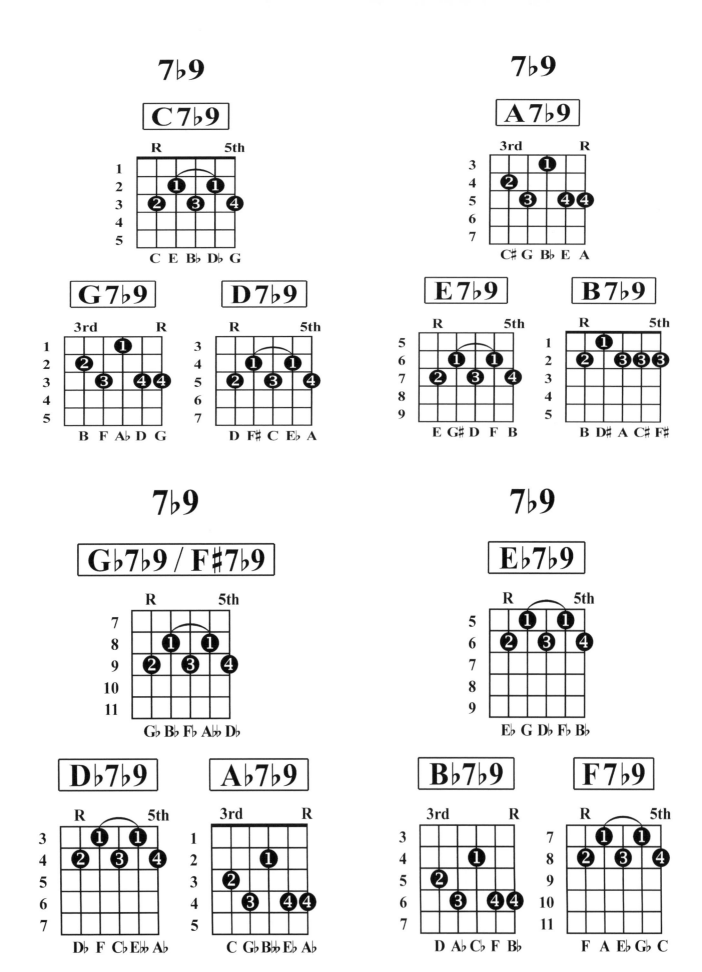

20

7#9

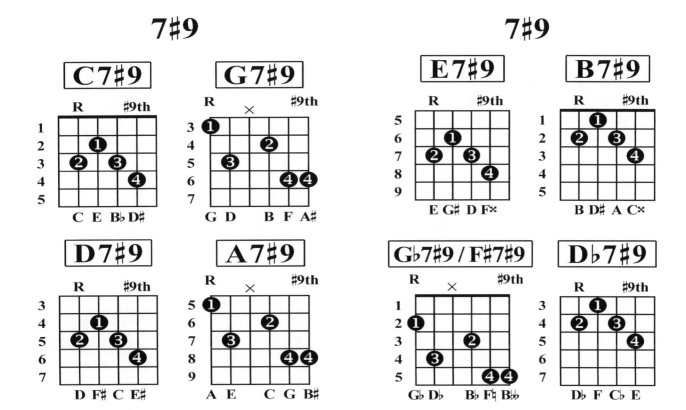

7#9

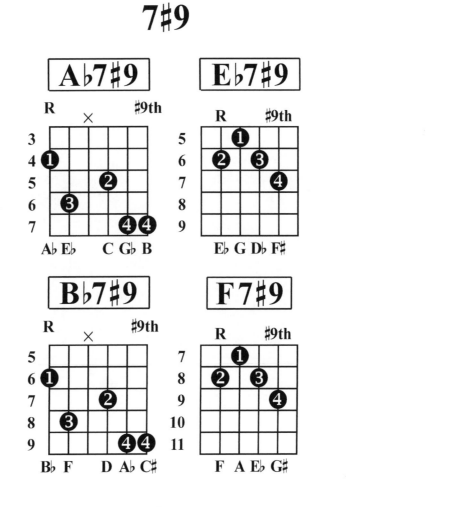

21

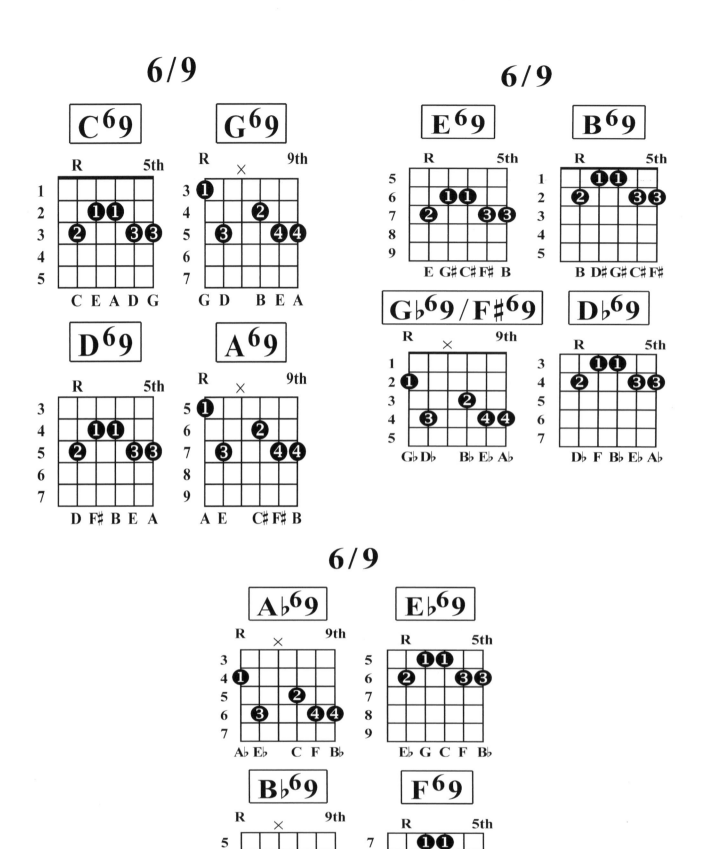

22

Major 9th

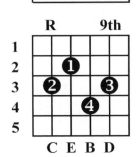

Major 9th

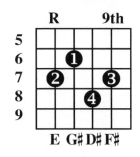

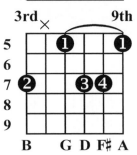

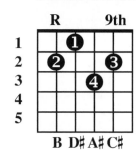

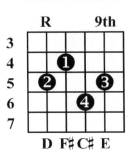

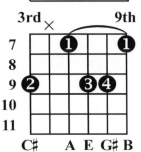

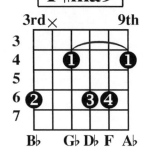

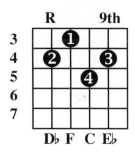

Major 9th

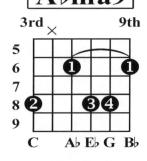

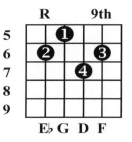

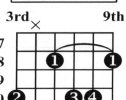

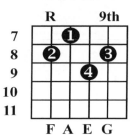

Minor 9th

Minor 9th

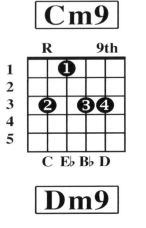

Cm9

R   9th

1   ①
2
3   ②   ③ ④
4
5

C E♭ B♭ D

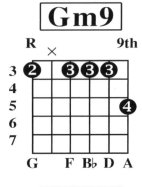

Gm9

R   ✕   9th

3   ②   ③ ③ ③
4
5   ④
6
7

G   F B♭ D A

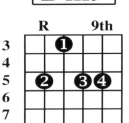

Dm9

R   9th

3   ①
4
5   ②   ③ ④
6
7

D F C E

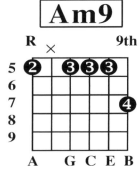

Am9

R   ✕   9th

5   ②   ③ ③ ③
6
7   ④
8
9

A   G C E B

Minor 9th

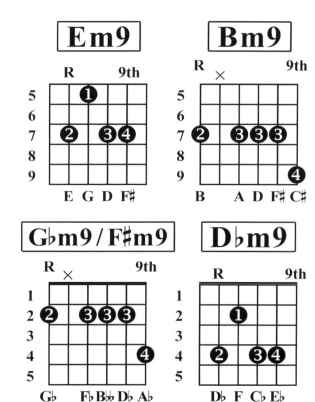

Em9

R   9th

5   ①
6
7   ②   ③ ④
8
9

E G D F#

Bm9

R   ✕   9th

5
6
7   ②   ③ ③ ③
8
9   ④

B   A D F# C#

G♭m9 / F#m9

R   ✕   9th

1
2   ②   ③ ③ ③
3
4   ④
5

G♭   F♭ B♭♭ D♭ A♭

D♭m9

R   9th

1
2   ①
3
4   ②   ③ ④
5

D♭ F C♭ E♭

Minor 9th

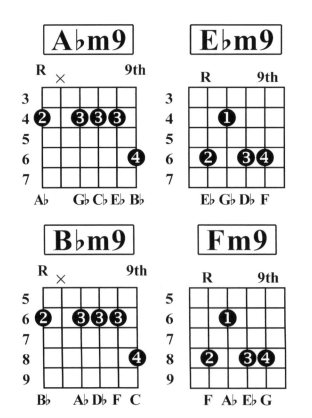

A♭m9

R   ✕   9th

3
4   ②   ③ ③ ③
5
6   ④
7

A♭   G♭ C♭ E♭ B♭

E♭m9

R   9th

3
4   ①
5
6   ②   ③ ④
7

E♭ G♭ D♭ F

B♭m9

R   ✕   9th

5
6   ②   ③ ③ ③
7
8   ④
9

B♭   A♭ D♭ F C

Fm9

R   9th

5
6   ①
7
8   ②   ③ ④
9

F A♭ E♭ G

24

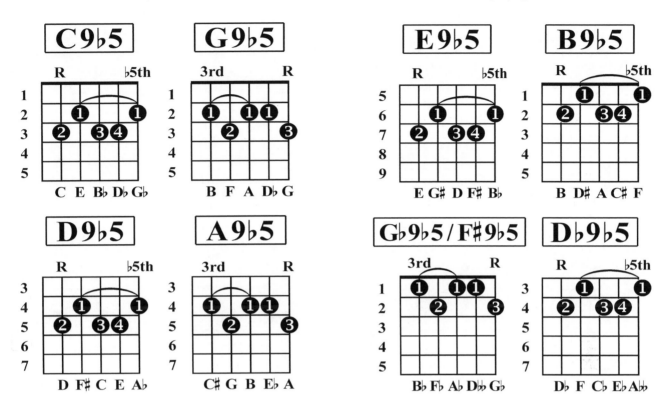

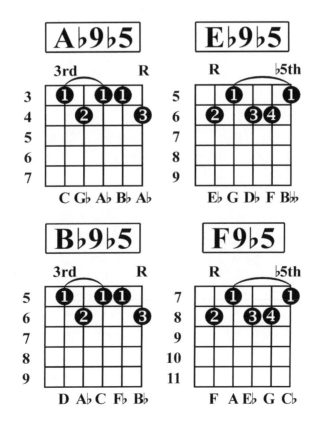

9♯5

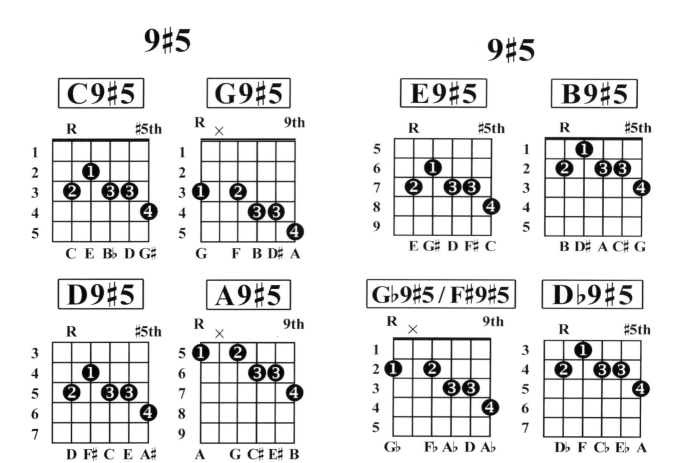

9♯5

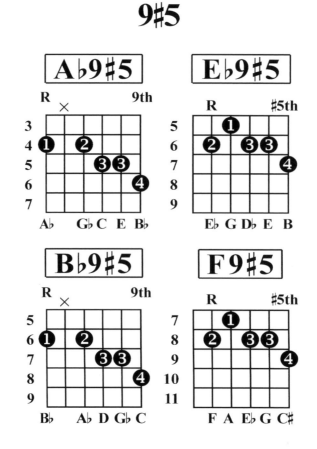

Eleventh

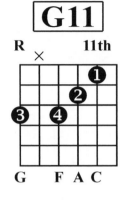

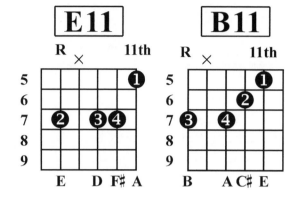

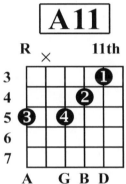

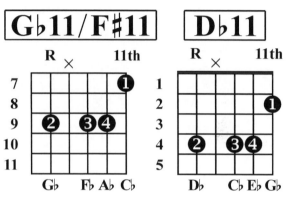

Eleventh

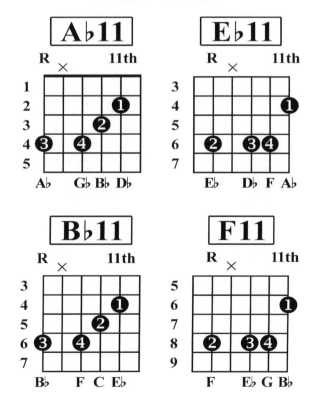

27

Augmented 11

CAug11
```
      R              #11th
1 |---|---|---|---|---|
2 |---|---| 1 |---| 1 |
3 | 2 |---|---| 3 | 4 |
4 |---|---|---|---|---|
5 |---|---|---|---|---|
   C   E   Bb  D   F#
```

GAug11
```
      R   ×          #11th
1 |---|---|---|---|---|
2 |---|---|---| 1 | 1 |
3 | 2 |---| 3 |---|---|
4 |---|---|---|---|---|
5 |---|---|---|---|---|
   G       F   A   C#
```

DAug11
```
      R              #11th
3 |---|---|---|---|---|
4 |---|---| 1 |---| 1 |
5 | 2 |---|---| 3 | 4 |
6 |---|---|---|---|---|
7 |---|---|---|---|---|
   D   F#  C   E   G#
```

AAug11
```
      R   ×          #11th
3 |---|---|---|---|---|
4 |---|---|---| 1 | 1 |
5 | 2 |---| 3 |---|---|
6 |---|---|---|---|---|
7 |---|---|---|---|---|
   A       G   B   D#
```

Augmented 11

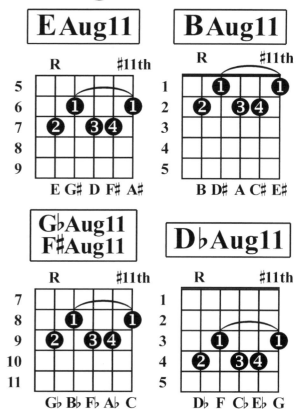

EAug11
```
      R              #11th
5 |---|---|---|---|---|
6 |---|---| 1 |---| 1 |
7 | 2 |---|---| 3 | 4 |
8 |---|---|---|---|---|
9 |---|---|---|---|---|
   E   G#  D   F#  A#
```

BAug11
```
      R              #11th
1 |---| 1 |---|---| 1 |
2 | 2 |---| 3 | 4 |---|
3 |---|---|---|---|---|
4 |---|---|---|---|---|
5 |---|---|---|---|---|
   B   D#  A   C#  E#
```

GbAug11 / F#Aug11
```
      R              #11th
7 |---|---|---|---|---|
8 |---|---| 1 |---| 1 |
9 | 2 |---|---| 3 | 4 |
10|---|---|---|---|---|
11|---|---|---|---|---|
   Gb  Bb  Fb  Ab  C
```

DbAug11
```
      R              #11th
1 |---|---|---|---|---|
2 |---|---|---|---|---|
3 |---|---| 1 |---| 1 |
4 | 2 |---|---| 3 | 4 |
5 |---|---|---|---|---|
   Db  F   Cb  Eb  G
```

Augmented 11

AbAug11
```
      R   ×          #11th
1 |---|---|---|---|---|
2 |---|---|---|---|---|
3 |---|---|---| 1 | 1 |
4 | 2 |---| 3 |---|---|
5 |---|---|---|---|---|
   Ab      Gb  Bb  D
```

EbAug11
```
      R              #11th
5 |---| 1 |---|---| 1 |
6 | 2 |---| 3 | 4 |---|
7 |---|---|---|---|---|
8 |---|---|---|---|---|
9 |---|---|---|---|---|
   Eb  G   Db  F   A
```

BbAug11
```
      R   ×          #11th
5 |---|---|---| 1 | 1 |
6 | 2 |---| 3 |---|---|
7 |---|---|---|---|---|
8 |---|---|---|---|---|
9 |---|---|---|---|---|
   Bb      Ab  C   E
```

FAug11
```
      R              #11th
7 |---| 1 |---|---| 1 |
8 | 2 |---| 3 | 4 |---|
9 |---|---|---|---|---|
10|---|---|---|---|---|
11|---|---|---|---|---|
   F   A   Eb  G   B
```

Thirteenth

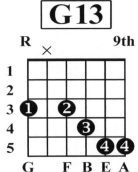

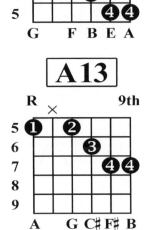

Thirteenth

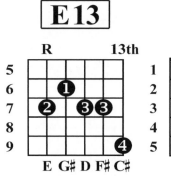

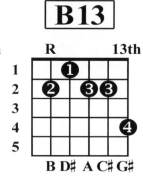

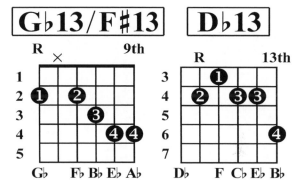

Thirteenth

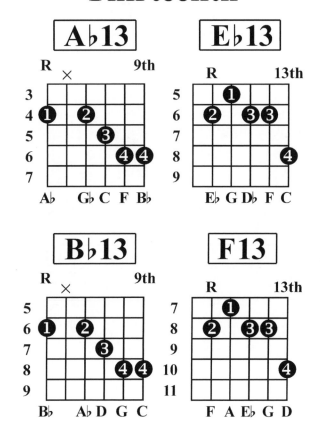

13♭9

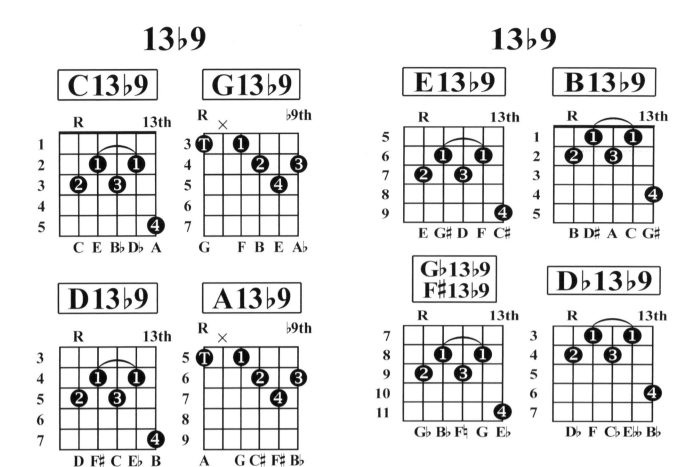

13♭9

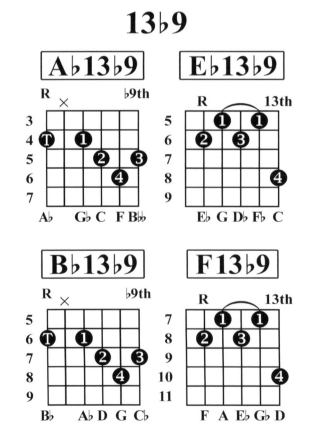

Major 13th

Major 13th

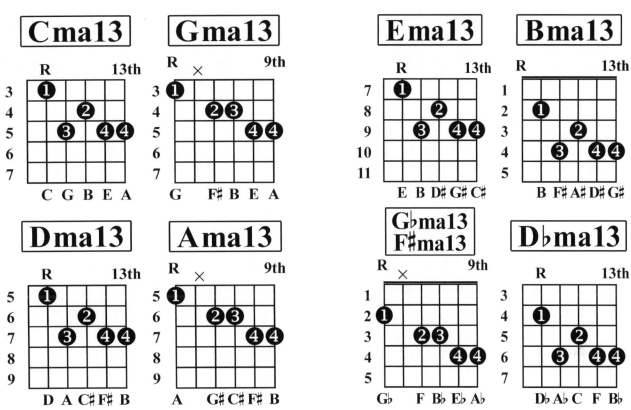

Major 13th

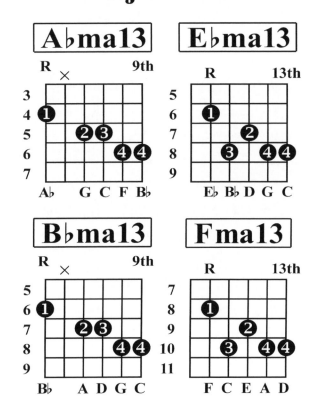

Mel Bay Jazz Guitar Chord and Theory Books

7-String Jazz Guitar Chord Chart (W. Bay)

21st Century Chords for Guitar (Bloom)

Achieving Guitar Artistry - Triads (W. Bay)

Bass Line Basics for Guitar (Chapman)

Coltrane Changes (C. Christiansen)

Comping the Blues (Vignola)

Complete Book of Harmony, Theory and Voicing (Willmott)

Complete Book of Harmonic Extensions for Guitar (Willmott)

Creative Comping Concepts for Jazz Guitar (Boling)

Deluxe Encyclopedia of Guitar Chords/Case Size (W. Bay)

Deluxe Encyclopedia of Guitar Chords/Full Size (W. Bay)

Deluxe Encyclopedia of Guitar Chord Progressions (Rector)

Drop 2 Concept for Guitar (Chapman)

George Van Eps Harmonic Mechanisms for Guitar Vol. 1

George Van Eps Harmonic Mechanisms for Guitar Vol. 2

George Van Eps Harmonic Mechanisms for Guitar Vol. 3

Guitar Fingerboard Harmony (McGuire)

Guitar Journals: Chords (W. Bay)

In the Pocket: Playing in the Groove (C. Christiansen)

Jazz Band Rhythm Guitar (Forman)

Jazz Guitar Chord Chart (W. Bay)

Jazz Guitar Chords Made Easy (W. Bay)

Jazz Gutar Essentials: Gig Savers Complete Edition (C. Christiansen)

Jazz Guitar Photo Chords (C. Christiansen)

Jazz Guitar Chord Substitution Wall Chart (C. Christiansen)

Jazz Guitar Chord Workout (C. Christiansen)

Jazz Guitar Comping (Andrew Green)

Jazz Chords for Rock Guitarists (Malone)

Joe Pass Guitar Chords

Modern Chords (Juris)

Modern Chord Technique (George M. Smith)

Playing the Blues: Blues Rhythm Guitar USC Curriculum (Trovato and Stoubis)

Quartal Harmony and Voicings for Guitar (Floyd)

Voice Motion (Haage)

WWW.MELBAY.COM

Made in the USA
Coppell, TX
03 March 2023

13709044R00020